Go Out in JOY
FESTIVE POSTLUDES FOR PIANO

ISBN 978-1-4584-2104-3

Harold Flammer
MUSIC

A DIVISION OF SHAWNEE PRESS, INC.
EXCLUSIVELY DISTRIBUTED BY HAL LEONARD CORPORATION

In Australia Contact:
Hal Leonard Australia Pty. Ltd.
4 Lentara Court
Cheltenham, Victoria, 3192 Australia
Email: ausadmin@halleonard.com.au

T0195285

Visit Shawnee Press Online at
www.shawneepress.com

AND CAN IT BE?

Dedicated to Hubert Bishop, Minister
Prison Ministry, Easley First Baptist Church

Arranged by
CAROLYN HAMLIN (ASCAP)

Words by CHARLES WESLEY
Music by THOMAS CAMPBELL

I STAND AMAZED IN THE PRESENCE
(My Savior's Love)

Arranged by
CINDY BERRY (ASCAP)

Words and Music by
CHARLES H. GABRIEL

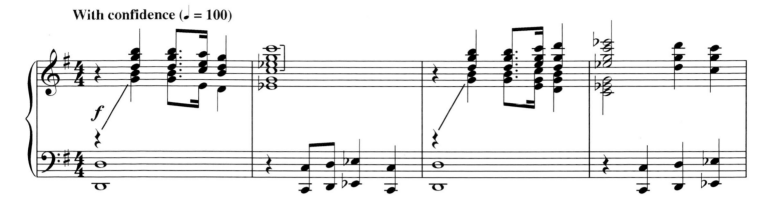

CROWN HIM WITH MANY CROWNS

Arranged by
BRAD NIX (ASCAP)

Words by MATTHEW BRIDGES and GODFREY THRING
Music by GEORGE JOB ELVEY

Fast, with a crisp rhythm (♩ = 132-138)

GOD OF GRACE AND GOD OF GLORY

Arranged by
PAMELA M. ROBERTSON

Words by HARRY EMERSON FOSDICK
Music by JOHN HUGHES

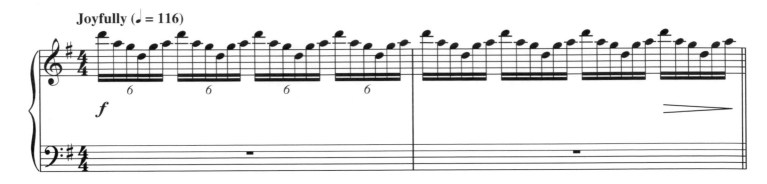

18

I KNOW WHOM I HAVE BELIEVED

Arranged by
HOJUN LEE

Words by DANIEL W. WHITTLE
Based on II Timothy 1:12
Music by JAMES McGRANAHAN

JESUS LOVES ME

Arranged by
VICKI TUCKER COURTNEY (ASCAP)

Words by ANNA B. WARNER
Music by WILLIAM B. BRADBURY

JOYFUL, JOYFUL, WE ADORE THEE

Arranged by
JAMES KOERTS (BMI)

Words by HENRY VAN DYKE
Music by LUDWIG VAN BEETHOVEN,
melody from *Ninth Symphony*
Adapted by EDWARD HODGES

Slower, with expression (♩ = 120)

LOVE DIVINE, ALL LOVES EXCELLING

Arranged by
PAMELA M. ROBERTSON

Words by CHARLES WESLEY
Music by JOHN ZUNDEL

With a jazzy feel

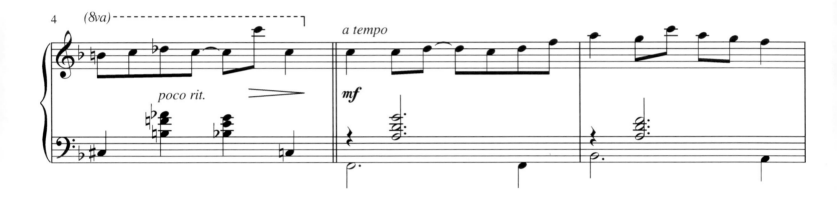

O WORSHIP THE KING

Arranged by
ALEX-ZSOLT (ASCAP)

Words by ROBERT GRANT
Music attributed to JOHANN MICHAEL HAYDN

POSTLUDE ON "HYFRYDOL"

(Jesus, What a Friend for Sinners)

Dedicated to my daughter, Terry Batson
Choral Director, Gettys Middle School, Easley, SC
Accompanist, Music Makers, Easley First Baptist Church

Arranged by
CAROLYN HAMLIN (ASCAP)

Words by J. WILBUR CHAPMAN
Music by ROWLAND H. PRICHARD

POSTLUDE ON "NETTLETON"
(Come, Thou Fount of Every Blessing)

Arranged by
JAMES KOERTS (BMI)

Words by ROBERT ROBINSON
Music from John Wyeth's *Repository of Sacred Music*

PRAISE TO THE LORD, THE ALMIGHTY

Arranged by
VICKI TUCKER COURTNEY (ASCAP)

Words by JOACHIM NEANDER
Translated by CATHERINE WINKWORTH
Music from *Erneuerten Gesangbuch*

LEAD ON, O KING ETERNAL

Arranged by
PAMELA M. ROBERTSON

Words by ERNEST W. SHURTLEFF
Welsh Folk Melody
Music from Evan's *Hymnau a Thonau*

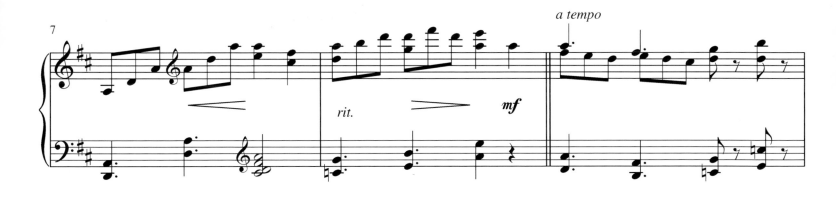